RIGHTS FOR ANIMALS?

DEIRDRE ROCHFORD

SEA-TO-SEA
Mankato Collingwood London

This edition first published in 2006 by
Sea-to-Sea Publications
1980 Lookout Drive
North Mankato
Minnesota 56003

Library of Congress Cataloging-in-Publication Data

Rochford, Deirdre.
    Rights for animals? / by Deirdre Rochford.
      p. cm. — (Viewpoints)
    Originally published: New York: Franklin Watts, 1997. (Viewpoints)
    Includes index.
    ISBN 1-932889-55-8
      1. Animal rights—Juvenile literature. I. Title. II. Viewpoints (Franklin Watts, inc)

HV4708.R625 2005
179'.3—dc22

                                    2004062516

9 8 7 6 5 4 3 2

Published by arrangement with the Watts Publishing Group Ltd, London

Picture credits:
b=bottom, t=top, r=right, l=left:
The Body Shop: 15b; *The Bridgeman Art Library*: p.4, 5t, 7b; *Bruce Coleman*: Dr. Inigo Everson p.7t, 13b; Hans Reinhard p.17l; Stephen J. Krasemann p.20bl; Erwin and Peggy Bauer 20br; George McCarthy p.21b; Norman Myers p.22b; John Shaw p.23b; 27b; Jane Burton p.28t; Dr. Eckart Pott p.29t; *Environmental Picture Library*: Pete Addis cover and p.10t; Mike Jackson p.14; 17r; Stephen Whitehorne p.20t; Paul Glendell p.26r; Andrew Testa p.27t; Eye Ubiquitous: 10b; Paul Prestidge p.11; Robert Harding: pp. 13t, 28b; Adam Woolfitt pp. 6b, 19t; Hugh Routledge p.18t; Shona Wood p.18b; *The Hutchison Library*: Jesco von Puttkamer p.6t; Jeremy A. Horner p.9t; David Cuverd p.16b; Edward Parker p.29b; *Panos Pictures*: 5b, 15t; Eric Miller 23r; Betty Press 22r; *RSPCA*: 9b, 16t, 25(both); Alban Donohoe 8l; Wayne Gray 24l; Nigel Rolstone 21t; *Rex Features*: 12l; *Today:* p.19b; Jenson p.26l; *Frank Spooner:* 12r; *Trip/T. Fisher*: 24b; *Zefa*: 8r

Quotation credits (given from the top of a page beginning with the left-hand column):
p.4 1 Stephen Budiansky, *Covenant of the Wild: Why Animals Chose Domesticity*, 1994; 2 Genesis 1:28, *The Bible*
p.5 1 Lynne Truss, *The Times*, 1993; 2 Tom Regan, *The Case for Animal Rights*, 1983; 3 American Society for the Prevention of Cruelty to Animals, spokesman, 1995
p.6 1 Harvey A. Feit, McMaster University, Canada, 1995; 2 Sarah Dunant, *The Trouble With Animals*, BBC TV, 1995; 3 David Street, *Fishing in Wild Places*, 1989
p.7 1 Dan and Karen Trotter, *Woman's Hour*, BBC Radio 4, 1995; 2 Andrew Ottaway, a whale conservationist, 1995; 3 World Wide Fund for Nature, 1996
p.8 1 Compassion in World Farming, 1995; 2 Delia Smith, *Complete Cookery Course*, 1978
p.9 Michael Kefler, Chief Executive, National Council of Shechita Boards, 1996
p.10 The Vegetarian Society, 1995
p.11 1 Carla Lane, writer of TV programs *Butterflies* and *Bread*; 2 Alan Owen, small part-time farmer, *Private Eye*, October 6, 1995
p.12 1 Chief Seattle of the Suquamish tribe in a letter to the President of the United States, 1855; 2 People for the Ethical Treatment of Animals campaign, USA, 1980s; 3 *Trapper and Predator Caller* magazine, USA, 1989

p.13 1 *The Facts About Fur*, Fur Education Council, 1995
p.14 1 *New York Times* advertisement, 1980; 2 Charles Darwin, naturalist, (1809-82)
p.15 1 British Association for the Advancement of Science, 1990; 2 British Union for the Abolition of Vivisection, 1995; 3 Andrew N. Rowan and Franklin M. Loew, *The Animal Research Controversy*, Tufts University School of Veterinary Medicine, 1995
p.16 1 Jessica Szymczyk, *Newsweek* 1995; 2 Michael Robinson, zoologist, 1994
p.17 1 John Bryant, *Fettered Kingdoms*; 2 The Guide Dogs for the Blind Association advertisement, 1995; 3 Robin Page, presenter of *One Man and His Dog*, BBC TV, 1995
p.18 1 David Nicholson, UK racehorse trainer, *The Duke*, 1995; 2 Action Against the Grand National; 3 Richard Pitman, *Turf Accounts, a Connoisseur's Racing Anthology*, Gollancz Witherby, 1995
p.19 People for the Ethical Treatment of Animals, *Greyhound Racing: Death in the Fast Lane*
p.20 1 Charles Dickens, novelist, (1812-70); 2 Hunt Saboteur Association, www.hsa.environweb.org, 19:9:03; 3 The League Against Cruel Sports, *Foxes and Foxhunting*, 1995; 4 Cameron Evans, secretary, Hunt Saboteurs Association
p.21 2 David Bellamy, conservationist, 1993;
p.22 *Care for the Wild News*, 1995
p.23 1 Michael Kock, Zimbabwean National Parks vet, 1993; 2 Nelson Mandela, from his speech posted on The Humane Society of the United States' website, www.hsus.org, 19:9:03; 3 *LifeWatch* magazine, 1995
p.24 1 London Zoo, 1995; 2 Brian Davies, founder of the International Fund for Animal Welfare
p.25 1 Julie Allday, RSPCA, 1995; 2 M. J. G. Bowman, *Connecticut Journal of International Law*, 1989; 3 The American Society for the Prevention of Cruelty to Animals, 1995
p.26 1 M. Leepson, Congressional Quarterly, 1991; 2 from statements signed by the animal rights group The Justice Department issued through the Animal Liberation Front Press Office, 1994
p.27 1 Michael Sissons, *The Spectator*, September 2, 1995; 2 American Society for the Prevention of Cruelty to Animals, 1995
p.28 1 George Orwell, *Animal Farm*, 1945; 2 Melanie Phillips, *The Trouble with Animals*, BBC TV, 1995; 3 Buddha, 566- 486BC
p.29 1 Bertrand Russell, philosopher, (1872-1970); 2 Tom Regan, author of *The Case for Animal Rights*, 1983. .

Contents

King of the beasts?

For two million years we were hunters; for ten thousand years we were farmers; for the last one hundred years we have been trying to deny it all... Stephen Budiansky, *Covenant of the Wild: Why Animals Chose Domesticity*

The great changes of the past two centuries—industrialization, population growth, and scientific and technological advancement—have completely transformed mankind's relationship with the animal kingdom. It is a development that many people have become increasingly concerned about.

Traditional thinking, influenced by religion, put animals firmly under mankind's power ("dominion").

Then God said Let us make man in our image...and let him have dominion over the fish of the sea and over the birds of the air, and over the cattle...and over every creeping thing that creeps upon the Earth... Genesis 1:28, *The Bible*

Charles Darwin's revolutionary books *On the Origin of Species* (1859) and *The Descent of Man* (1871) challenged this view. By claiming that humans evolved from the apes, through natural selection, Darwin made nonsense of the idea that humans were set apart from the rest of the animal kingdom. His ideas sparked off the kind of furious debate that people have about animal rights today.

▼ *A lost ideal? In Christianity's Garden of Eden, all creatures lived together in harmony but with humans definitely superior to animals.*

▲ *Darwin's theory that we are descended from apes was ridiculed by many people at the time but is now a generally accepted principle.*

66 *'Fish have rights' I read. Of course I laughed out loud. Rights to what? Fair trial? Freedom of expression? Abortion on demand?* 99
Lynne Truss, journalist

What are "animal rights"? The usual explanation of "rights" is a just claim to be treated a certain way by society, and to enjoy the benefits of that society. We must decide whether animals just have the right to be respected and treated kindly, or whether they have exactly the same rights as humans.

Some philosophers believe that animals do have the same rights as humans and that it is "speciesism," a prejudice like racism or sexism, to think that we are more valuable than any animal.

66 *(If) it is wrong to treat weaker human beings, especially those who are lacking in normal human intelligence, as tools…or commodities, then it cannot be right, therefore, to treat animals as tools…and the like.* 99 *Tom Regan, The Case for Animal Rights*

Others argue that rights are unique to humans because only humans have free will, the ability to reason, and make choices. Some people feel that it is wrong to talk of animal rights in a world where many people do not yet have basic rights.

However, most people can agree that animal rights should extend as far as to protect animals from unnecessary cruelty.

66 *We're not an animal rights organization. Animal rights is a loaded term in the U.S. We're a humane animal protection organization, lobbying for better treatment for animals.* 99
American Society for the Prevention of Cruelty to Animals

The theory behind animal rights is only a starting point. The issues become far more complicated when applied to the practical realities of the modern world. This book explores some of these issues and their implications for the animal-rights debate.

▼ *The modern world is overcrowded and heavily industrialized. Humans have such dominance in the world that there can be no "natural" balance now between mankind and animals.*

A natural resource?

Some people still live in the way that our forefathers did, hunting and scratching a living from the land. Unlike most of the modern world, their relationship with animals has remained unchanged by the advances of the 20th and 21st century.

❝ The Cree Indians have built their whole culture on killing. The irony is they have no problem accepting their equality with animals. ❞
Harvey A. Feit, McMaster University, Hamilton, Canada

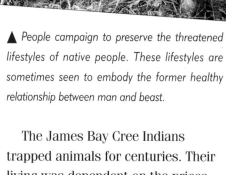

▲ People campaign to preserve the threatened lifestyles of native people. These lifestyles are sometimes seen to embody the former healthy relationship between man and beast.

The James Bay Cree Indians trapped animals for centuries. Their living was dependent on the prices fur fetched. When the Western world turned against the fur trade, their way of life collapsed. The Inuit were affected by the antisealing campaign in the same way.

❝ Only now are they beginning to recover from the effects. In their case, animal rights meant the loss of human ones. ❞ The Trouble With Animals, BBC TV

People with traditional lifestyles are often envied for their "pure" lives,

◀ The sea turns red during the Grindadrap whale hunt. Such scenes horrify, but can they be justified by our need for whale products?

▶ It was once thought that the fish stocks would never dry up—now it looks like they may well do.

which are close to nature. Yet, at the same time, modern society has turned against hunting peoples. It is hard to see where a respect for tradition becomes a toleration of cruelty.

❝ Some men stood in the boats and thrust their spears into the whales. Some men were even trying to ride the whales into the shore. The waters rapidly began to turn crimson. ❞
David Street, describing the Grindadrap, the Faroe Islanders' whale hunt, Fishing in Wild Places

The violent nature of the Faroese whale hunt disgusts many people. But the Faroese defend their right to hunt whales. They say that they depend on the sea, and everything in it, for their living.

❝ The Faroese really do live with their environment and take a sustainable harvest of pilot whales. The argument has to be made in favor of traditional hunts. ❞
Dan and Karen Trotter, Faroese islanders

The debate against these hunting peoples is not just about violence but is also about where the line is drawn between harvesting nature's sustainable resources and depleting them for profit. The whaling nations argue that there are enough whales to support their industry. The International Whaling Commission imposed a ban on commercial whaling beginning in 1985, but endorsed whaling by some indigenous communities for their survival.

❝ I'm very depressed about it. In a way the conservationists have been guilty of hyping their own success. People think the whaling issue is clear-cut when it could yet be lost. ❞
Andrew Ottaway, a whale conservationist

The antiwhaling lobby has one big advantage in the debate: whales are huge intelligent animals and people feel very emotional about their plight. Fish do not inspire the same emotion but overfishing has also become a problem. The extent of commercial fishing means that the world's fish stocks are disappearing fast.

❝ Unless steps are taken to control the overfishing of the North Sea, we estimate favorites like cod and haddock will become extinct. ❞
World Wide Fund for Nature

Demand for fish is now so great that it cannot be met through a sustainable harvest of fish. Increased fish farming may now be necessary to protect the falling wild stocks.

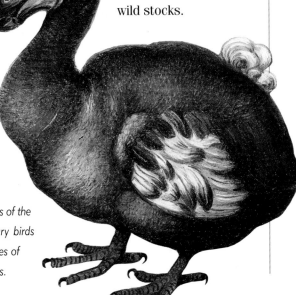

▶ The saying "dead as a dodo" reminds us of the dangers of extinction. These extraordinary birds were wiped out by 1800. One of the causes of their extinction was overhunting by humans.

Is farming cruel?

How do farmed animals fare in today's world? In Europe, furious protests began in the UK in 1995 over exports of live cattle to European countries that require long road trips, and demonstrations at British docks continued in 2003.

" In the UK, the rest of the European Union, and beyond, hundreds of millions of farm animals are being kept in conditions which deprive them of even basic behavioral needs. "
Compassion in World Farming

Modern farming methods have been developed to deal with the huge demand for animal produce. In the U.S., nearly 10 billion animals are slaughtered each year for their meat. In the UK, some 883 million are slaughtered annually for food, including about 20 million sheep and lambs, 14 million pigs, 4 million cattle, and 720 million broiler chickens. The farming community is pressurized by consumers to produce huge quantities of food at low prices.

" Once upon a time chicken was a luxury. It is a credit to our farmers that they have put chicken within the reach of everyone at what, in these days, is a very reasonable price. "
Delia Smith, food writer

▲ This goose is being force-fed to expand its liver to make pâté de foie gras. Are animals paying the price for our luxury food?

◄ The pigs at this "Freedom Foods" approved farm are treated humanely. Such farms are good for animals but may well be bad for food prices.

▲ *Battery hens are often packed in cages where they cannot stretch their wings, but these farms respond to the huge demand for eggs and chicken.*

With pressure on farmers from consumers, it is perhaps not surprising that farm animals are sometimes treated more like manufactured products than living creatures.

But intensive farming leads to a variety of problems: keeping animals indoors can lead to lameness and mastitis (sore udders) in dairy cattle and bone fractures for caged hens; the use of superovulation to produce multiple births in cattle can lead to problems at delivery.

Even natural farming methods can bring problems. Moving livestock around the UK helped spread "foot-and-mouth" disease in 2001.

Religious practices raise a different kind of problem. In many countries, animals are legally required to be stunned with an electric shock before they are slaughtered. To do so goes against the beliefs of Muslims and Jews, which require that animals killed under Halal (Muslim) or Shechita (Jewish) procedures should not be stunned first. Religious and cultural ways should be respected, but are animals suffering for our beliefs?

66 *There is scientific evidence showing that shechita is as humane as any other slaughter technique.* 99 *National Council of Shechita Boards*

Farming welfare standards and expectations differ throughout the world. This, too, can cause problems. In Denmark in the early 1980s when conditions were improved for hens, eggs produced in worse systems were then imported because they were cheaper. In the UK, public opinion has turned against transporting animals for long distances, only to be slaughtered at the end. But the French public still want their meat fresh, which means transporting animals live. Perhaps the answer is a world where no one eats meat.

▼ *Veal calves are sometimes raised in restricting veal crates and fed on an exclusive milk diet. They are also exported live and the long journeys overseas are thought to be very stressful.*

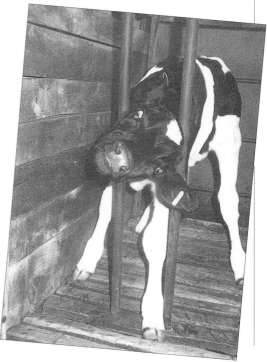

Should we eat meat?

The average person in the West will consume 1,000 chickens, 30 sheep, and 20 pigs in their lifetime. But if meat is not strictly necessary for our survival, why eat it?

" Most people become vegetarian because they believe it is wrong to slaughter animals for food. "
The Vegetarian Society

A U.S. poll in 2003 found that 2.8 percent of Americans were vegetarians who eat no meat or fish, and 6 percent who eat fish but no meat. By 2003, 5 percent of Britons were vegetarian. Young people in particular are becoming vegetarian.

Myths that vegetarianism is unhealthy have been shown to be untrue. Research on heart disease and cancer suggests that a vegetarian diet may even be healthier. However, others say that a vegetarian lifestyle goes against our omnivorous nature.

Some people avoid eating meat because they worry about the quality produced by intensive farming. From 1996–99, British beef was removed from sale worldwide because of fears that "mad cow disease" (BSE), a fatal disease of the nervous system, might infect humans. British cows were infected after controls on cattle feed were relaxed. Over 80 Britons are believed to have died since 1985 of CJD, the human form of BSE, after eating infected meat.

▲ The traditional Western meal of "meat and potatoes" seems to be disappearing as more people lose their taste for red meat.

▲ Fish is acceptable to some who follow a vegetarian lifestyle.

Vegetarians do not eat meat, poultry, game, or fish. Nor do they eat slaughter byproducts, although sometimes these are less easily spotted. For instance, gelatin, which comes from animal bones, is used in ice cream, candy, and dairy products. Animal fats may be present in cookies, cakes, and margarines. Cheese, unless specifically vegetarian, is usually made with rennet, which is taken from calves' stomach lining. The real stumbling block for many vegetarians, though, is milk.

66 *It's no good crying out against the (calf export) trade if you are going to have milk.* **99** *Carla Lane, writer and animal welfare campaigner*

The only truly vegetarian way of life is vegan (eating no animal or dairy products), but this is difficult and possibly unhealthy. Many people feel that a less strict form of vegetarianism—perhaps, for example, still eating fish and dairy products—is acceptable and a worthwhile reduction in the consumption of animal products.

Some people think breeding animals for meat is an inefficient way to feed the world when 11 million children die of hunger each year. For every 22lb (10kg) of grain fed to animals, only 2lb (1kg) is converted into meat. On average, a meat-eater's diet uses twice as much land as a vegetarian's, and good land is scarce throughout the world.

A world devoted to growing grain and vegetables would cause problems, too: the goodness in soils could quickly be used up by intensive farming; chemical fertilizers can be damaging to the environment. The best organic alternative to fertilizers is animal manure from keeping animals inside over the winter.

66 *I am at a loss to see how vegetarians would maintain their food supplies without the millions of tons of s**t produced by the overwintering of beasts.* **99** *Alan Owen, part-time farmer*

And the weather is uncontrollable. A drought in Eastern Australia in 2002, the worst since 1788, destroyed crops and cost the rural economy A$ 1 billion. It seems that it is not yet possible for the world to be vegan.

▼ *Many areas of rural beauty throughout the world are a result of the tradition of farming animals. What would happen to these areas if the whole world became vegetarian?*

Vanity, all is vanity?

Some people who do not eat meat also refuse to wear leather. Others won't eat meat, but do wear leather. This could be called hypocritical. If you are going to kill an animal for food, isn't it better to use every last scrap of it? The Native Americans thought this way. They were horrified that the incoming settlers killed the buffalo herds for their skin alone.

❝ *I have seen a thousand rotting buffaloes on the prairie, left by the white man.* **❞** *Chief Seattle of the Suquamish tribe in a letter to the President of the United States, 1855*

The wearing of fur and other exotic animal skins such as crocodile has become a controversial issue. These animals are only killed for their skin. The more exotic the animal the more valuable their skin.

❝ *I'd rather go naked than wear fur.* **❞** *People for the Ethical Treatment of Animals campaign*

◀ *Dressed to thrill or dressed to kill? The fur trade was rocked by powerful advertising campaigns started by those protesting against the fur trade.*

The antifur campaign shook the traditional fur markets. In the U.S., sales fell from nearly $2 billion per year in 1987 to a mere $500 million by 1999.

❝ *The European market fell in less than three years from the top consuming region to an area where furs are now looked upon with distaste.* **❞** *Trapper and Predator Caller magazine, USA*

Wearing fur has largely become socially unacceptable in the UK, where fur farming was banned in 2003. But people wearing fur coats are often seen on the streets of cities like Milan, and new markets for fur have appeared in places like Korea.

▼ *Russia is one of the countries where a fur coat is still a status symbol.*

eyes, mouth, and hair, from suntan lotion to perfume—are often made from animal products. It could be argued that these products are not essential, but demand for them suggests that people feel otherwise. Cosmetic departments are usually right at the heart of a store, and a whole new industry has grown up around cosmetics for men.

The production of cosmetics without animal ingredients has become a huge industry. Unfortunately, that does not solve the problem because the law requires that all new ingredients in cosmetics must be tested on animals.

Can pain to animals be justified if it causes people to be out of pain?

If the demand for fur continues, perhaps fur farming is a more acceptable way to meet that demand than trapping animals in the wild. Most pelts (fur skins) come from fur farms now. Fur was originally worn for practical reasons—warmth—but with alternatives available, surely it is just vanity to wear it now?

66 *Wearing fur can be just as easily justified as wearing leather, or eating eggs, meat, cheese, and fish.* 99
Fur Education Council

One of the alternatives to fur is wool. But even wool is not free from debate. It does not involve killing any animals, but shearing is stressful for sheep and they would not shed their whole fleece in the wild.

Clothes are essential, but we "wear" animals in different ways. Cosmetics—which includes anything we put on our skin,

Kill or cure?

Vivisection is one of the most fiercely argued aspects of the animal rights debate. Advertisements such as the one above have raised public awareness of the vivisection issue and businesses and governments have had to respond accordingly.

Revlon no longer test their products on animals and Britain banned cosmetics tests in 1998, after the European Council of Ministers blocked a proposed Europe-wide ban. (A limited EU ban begins in 2009). The British law only stopped cosmetics experiments, not safety tests for household products. In the UK, nearly 3 million animals are still used in tests each year. In 1999, activists shut a farm breeding cats for medical tests in a long siege, which saw 350 arrests and cost the police $5.2 million.

The law demands that all new ingredients of any product must be tested to make sure that they are safe. Many of these tests have to be carried out on animals. These tests protect people from harmful products but at the expense of animal discomfort and often death.

Vivisection is also used in the progress of medicine.

I have all my life been a strong advocate for humanity to animals, and have done what I could in my writings to enforce this duty. I know that physiology cannot progress except by means of experiments on living animals, and I feel the deepest conviction that he who retards the progress of physiology commits a crime against mankind.
Charles Darwin, 19th-century naturalist

Anyone who has suffered from the following will have been treated by medicine developed as a result of research on animals: diabetes, asthma, cancer, polio, high blood pressure, kidney transplant, heart transplant, and hip replacement.

◄ *Animal experimentation was necessary for the development of this child's asthma inhaler. Is his life more important than the lives of those animals who died?*

▶ *It makes us uncomfortable to see pictures of experiments on animals, but are such experiments necessary evils for the progress of medicine?*

Modern surgery and life-support systems for premature babies were also developed through experiments on animals.

The British Association for the Advancement of Science states:

❝ *Continued research involving animals is essential for the conquest of many unsolved medical problems such as cancer, AIDS, and genetic, developmental, neurological, and psychiatric conditions.* ❞
British Association for the Advancement of Science

But not everyone believes that animal research has contributed to the advancement of medicine:

❝ *Today we are losing the battle against diseases such as cancer, heart disease, and AIDS, as millions are invested in misleading animal studies.* ❞ *British Union for the Abolition of Vivisection*

People are trying to develop alternatives to experiments on animals. Computer models can now be used in research, and living cells can be grown in "culture," for use in tests. The problem is that these methods have to be validated— shown to work reliably in different laboratories—and this takes time.

Some scientists do not think that any of these methods is enough on its own and that it is still necessary to look at what is happening in the whole living animal.

❝ *The national trend in the United States is toward the reduced use of animals in biomedical research, but there is little chance of completely replacing animals.* ❞ *Tufts University School of Veterinary Medicine*

How can we balance the need to relieve human suffering with the need to protect animals from unnecessary suffering?

◀ *Almost all cosmetic ingredients have been tested on animals at some stage in the past. However, companies like The Body Shop, who have built their reputation on being animal friendly, do not test any of their finished products or raw ingredients on animals.*

Man's best friend?

" *I've been a vegetarian since I was 13. I don't wear cosmetics. I won't buy or wear fur. I refuse to wear or use leather. And I absolutely love animals. I get angry when I hear the terrible things animal-rights groups say about how we supposedly treat laboratory animals.* **"**
Jessica Szymczyk

Jessica Szymczyk looks after the animals in a U.S. research laboratory. She thinks they are often better cared for than many pets, or "companion animals." In the UK, the Royal Society for the Prevention of Cruelty to Animals

▼ *Dogs make loving companions, they can provide comfort and can reduce stress levels in people. But some people ask "What is in it for the dog?" and want to see fewer pets.*

(RSPCA) is very concerned about the number of mistreated and abandoned pets. They have tried to increase awareness about the cost and responsibility of owning a pet "for life, and not just for Christmas," as one of their campaigns has put it.

There are 65 million pet dogs and 76 million cats kept as pets in the USA alone. Pets are now a big business worldwide:

" *What we in the United States spend on our dogs and cats amounts to a sum greater than the entire economy of medieval Europe.* **"**
Michael Robinson, zoologist

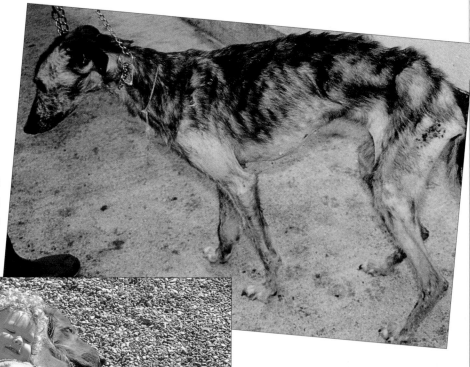

▲ *In the UK, the RSPCA receives a phone call every 26 seconds. Neglect is still their worst problem.*

Pet owners say that their animals are cherished companions, enjoying a better life than their wild cousins. It is a two-way bond, providing nourishment for both sides. Hospitals have taken this idea

▶▲ *Sheepdogs and guide dogs for the blind provide a worthy service to people. They are trained to go against their nature but are often well cared for in return. Are they exploited by people or is the relationship mutually beneficial?*

dogs and studying the effects of stress on working dogs. Guide dogs work hard. Their role is particularly difficult, since they have to be trained to go against their natural instincts. This is true of any animal trained to work for humans, but some people believe that animals actually enjoy work.

66 *I have long admired sheepdogs.... The bond between man and dog is wonderful to see. It is based on trust, dedication, and skill. The natural hunting instinct of the dog has been modified to herd.... The dogs love and need work; the shepherds depend on the dogs and it is a system of two way reliance.* **99**
One Man and His Dog, BBC TV

Animals used in these ways are providing invaluable service to people. Using animals for entertainment may be more difficult to justify.

further, by bringing in dogs to visit patients. Research has shown that stroking a dog can help reduce people's blood pressure. Some people think that we should not keep pets at all.

66 *I have not the slightest hesitation in saying that pet animals should be phased out of existence. My reason for this view is that pet animals are slaves and prisoners.* **99**
John Bryant, Fettered Kingdoms

If pets can be seen as slaves, what about working animals? Their contribution to our lives can be huge.

66 *'Sit—Stay—Down—Make an omelette.' The things we can't teach a dog to do, we teach the owner.* **99**
The Guide Dogs for the Blind Association advertisement

Providing dogs to act as people's eyes is only part of the work of Guide Dogs for the Blind. Other projects include solving sight problems in

A good sport?

In the developed world few animals are still used as working animals. However, many sports involving animals have developed from our working relationship with them.

Sport involves animals in different ways. Riding is one of the most popular sports, even if the child riding a pony on a trail seems a long way from the winner of the Kentucky Derby or the Grand National. It is arguable which has the harder life, a riding-school horse or a racehorse.

66 A racehorse is one of the most loved, and best looked after, of all animals. 99 David Nicholson, racehorse trainer

Running, for horses, is a response to danger. In the wild they go around obstacles rather than jump over them. So perhaps it is unnatural and stressful to expect them to take part in a rodeo, or show-jumping, eventing, polo, dressage, or racing. This is the view of those groups that campaign against horse racing.

66 Racing is cruel and degrading to horses. 99 Action Against the Grand National

Either horses and other animals perform because they are too scared not to—or because they want to. Those who work with animals say that training and performance come

▲ ▶ *The bond between horse and jockey is strong. Horses require a great deal of care but much is demanded of them in return.*

down to mutual trust between horse and rider.

66 What many regular race-goers fail to understand is the bond between horse and rider. The whole thing revolves around confidence from the saddle being transmitted to the horse. 99 Richard Pitman, A Connoisseur's Racing Anthology

But are people really interested in the animals in the race or the money to be made from it? Racing (including betting and breeding) is the sixth largest industry in the UK. A great deal of money is made from animal sports all around the world. In the USA, about $2 billion was wagered on greyhound races in the year 2000 at 50 tracks in 15 states, which attract around 15 million people annually.

66 *The natural speed and grace of greyhounds has been exploited for human benefit since the days of the Ancient Egyptians.... Modern dog racing has turned this...breed into a commodity for greyhound breeders and racetrack owners.* 99 *People for the Ethical Treatment of Animals*

A lot of money is riding on sports, with television deals, sponsors, and advertising. Animal welfare groups and those involved in sports are cooperating more than they used to to ensure that animals do not suffer through being pushed too hard.

▶ *Gambling on animal sports is a huge business.*

▼ *Are some animal sports more acceptable than others? Some people think that bullfighting is barbaric. Others see it as part of their lives and culture.*

A right to hunt?

Famous horse races like the UK's Grand National developed from foxhunting. People raced their hunt horses against their friends' for fun. Jump racing is still run under "National Hunt" rules.

Although we still hunt in the sea, on an individual level we no longer depend on hunting for our food. However, hunting—whether birds, mammals, such as foxes and deer, or fish—continues as a sport. In 2003, the U.S. had about 17 million hunters.

❝ *There is a passion for hunting deeply implanted in the human breast.* ❞ *Charles Dickens, 19th-century novelist*

Attitudes have changed since Dickens' day.

❝ *The only way to stop a foxhunt killing foxes is to sabotage it!* ❞ *Hunt Saboteurs Association*

▼ *Hunters keep the stuffed heads or sometimes feet of the animals that they have killed as trophies to show the variety and quantity of their kills. Some people find this practice unpleasant.*

▲ *Fishing is seen as one of the most peaceful sports, but those against fishing say that it is painful and distressing for the fish.*

▼ *Some see hunting as a way of being part of the natural order of things, with man pitted against the wild. Others see hunting as a pointless destruction of beautiful animals.*

Others feel that certain kinds of hunting are more deplorable than others. Some people that oppose foxhunting do not oppose sport-fishing even though research shows that fish feel pain.

Foxhunting with hounds was banned in Scotland in 2002, and in 2005, the ban extended to England and Wales.

❝Foxhunting has the same purpose as the now illegal pastimes of dogfighting, bear baiting, and cockfighting—to provide amusement for human beings. ❞ The League Against Cruel Sports

Groups against foxhunting argue that banning it altogether would save the lives of foxes:

❝We have been in existence for almost 30 years, and in that time thousands of lives have been saved. ❞ Hunt Saboteurs Association

Their view is challenged.

❝The abolition of foxhunting will not make a hap'orth [half-penny worth] of difference to animal welfare. Well over 200,000 foxes are killed in the UK every year by much worse methods than foxhunting. ❞ Richard Course, former chairman of the League Against Cruel Sports, Horse & Hound magazine

Hunters argue that we live in a world where, for better or worse, animals are controlled, and that hunting is a more natural method than snaring, gassing, or mangling animals under a car's wheels.

▲ ▶ Foxhunting is disapproved of by many. Those who live and work in the countryside often believe that it is a more humane way of culling foxes than snaring or trapping.

In the past few years, the arguments have moved from cruelty on to environmental issues. It is argued that country sports bring money and jobs into rural parts. They have shaped the countryside as we know it and value it today, preserving small woods, ponds, and wild ground that would have gone under the plow otherwise.

❝Rural Britain is not a theme park which has to be kept nice for weekends, regardless of the cost during the week. We live in a human-made and human-maintained landscape. The habitats within which our wildlife lives is shaped and cared for by the skills of rural people. The life of the countryside is dependent upon the livelihoods of the people who live there, not the prejudices of those who don't. ❞ Richard Burge, Chief Executive, Countryside Alliance

Throughout history, landowners' desire to hunt has provided areas of conserved beauty in the form of game parks. Ironically, blood sports have preserved animal habitats. Hunting people were arguably the first conservationists.

❝Without the conservation management provided by country shooting, all this beautiful countryside and everything that it contains, the flowers, the wildlife, and the songbirds would have disappeared a long time ago. ❞ David Bellamy, conservationist

A battle for survival?

Some animals are being hunted to extinction. The debate over "big game" hunting, particularly in Africa, is not just about the pain of the individual animal but about the survival of an entire species.

The discussion over the African elephant is an example of this debate. CITES (the Convention on International Trade in Endangered Species of Wild Fauna and Flora) lists the elephant on Appendix 1. This means that any trade in ivory, skin and meat is prohibited. Several southern African countries want to downgrade the elephant to Appendix 2. This would allow them to do some trade in skin and meat.

For some, the argument is simple. These people believe that the elephant must have full protection from any type of trade. They believe that the ivory ban saved the elephants from being wiped out and that to start the trade again would be unthinkable. They argue that the culling (selective killing) of elephants must stop. They believe that elephants will encourage tourism.

66 *There is an alternative to South Africa cruelly culling its extra elephants—realizing the potential for ecotourism.* **99** *Care For The Wild*

Others argue that the elephant is not endangered. They believe that it is better to teach local people to

▲ *Richard Leakey, a conservationist, burned ivory in Kenya as a protest against poaching.*

▼ *Life in Africa can be hard for people and animals alike. A balance must be found that suits both.*

▶ A black rhino has its horns removed by conservationists in Kenya to protect it from poachers. It is strange and sad that animals have to be mutilated to be protected.

value the elephants as a potential crop, rather than a threat to their existing crops. Tourism alone, they argue, is too fragile to support the elephants. Developing countries should be allowed to use trade in elephants to bring in funds.

66 *The old preservationist philosophy is no longer working. Beyond tourism, animals have got to start paying their own way. We're protecting them into extinction.* 99 *Michael Kock, Zimbabwean National Parks vet*

South Africa has been reviled by conservationists throughout the world for its policy of culling elephants in areas where they say there are too many. Former South African President Nelson Mandela once argued that South Africa needed all the money it could raise—even if this was from elephants. By 2002, however, he had changed his mind:

66 *If we do not do something to prevent [the killing of elephants], Africa's animals…will be lost to our world, and her children forever.* 99 *Nelson Mandela*

International legislation from CITES is sometimes ineffective. Perhaps the most notorious animal trade is the tiger industry. At the beginning of the 20th century there were

some 80,000 tigers in the wild, now there are about 5,000. Three species have disappeared since the 1950s.

66 *Across Asia the trade in tiger parts continues because of the Far Eastern traditional medicine culture. In 1990 a Taiwanese brewery imported 4,400lb of bones—more than 50 tigers—to support a yearly production of 100,000 bottles of tiger bone wine!* 99 *LifeWatch magazine*

The tiger is threatened by opposed human values ("We

think our medicine works" versus "We think your medicine methods are cruel"). How can we ensure that endangered species are fully protected? Perhaps the only way is to keep them away from humans, even if this means sacrificing their freedom in sanctuaries, reserves, and zoos.

▼ Ecotourism makes African animals profitable. This provides protection for animals and financial support for Africa.

How can we protect animals?

" In an ideal world, all living things would be able to live in their natural environment. However, this century we have seen the overpopulation of our planet by the human being and the struggle to survive has become virtually impossible for many other species. Captive breeding programs in zoos are, for many kinds of animals, the only hope left of avoiding extinction. " London Zoo

There are 10,000 zoos around the world. These can offer protection to many species and help to boost populations in the wild. Moreover, zoos can be educational, giving people a chance to see live animals.

Some people feel, however, that zoos are an outdated concept and that their main purpose is our entertainment.

" Zoos, for many species, are a jail for life. At the end of the day, they just provide work for zookeepers. " Brian Davies, founder of the International Fund for Animal Welfare

Some people feel that zoos are a way of protecting animals, particularly those in danger of extinction. Animals can also be protected by using the law.

Animal welfare and animal rights

▶ Zoos provide veterinary care for animals, as well as breeding stock for rare species.

pressure groups have persuaded governments to pass laws about the treatment of animals. The world's first animal protection organization was the Royal Society for the Prevention of Cruelty to Animals (RSPCA), founded in 1824 in the UK. The American branch, the ASPCa, is one of many similar groups that have

been organized to pursue the same aimsworldwide.

Legal protection for animals varies hugely throughout the world. Switzerland has had a comprehensive law since 1978; the Spanish Parliament rejected a

▼ *This polar bear is a long way from its icy home. TThe zoo is an unnatural environment.*

national animal welfare law in 1992; Israel introduced its first Animal Protection Act in 1994. In the UK, animal laws cover cruelty, experiments, slaughter, exhibitions (performing animals or animals in film), animal establishments, birds, markets, transit, game laws, and conservation.

> *Countries that do not have many humanitarian problems are more likely to have stronger animal protection laws. If a country is emerging from civil war, or having problems feeding its people, animal welfare comes way down the line.*
> RSPCA

As well as national legislation, animals in Europe are covered by laws of the European Parliament and Council. These laws mainly cover trade in animals. Conventions (formal meetings) have been set up to discuss the protection of animals. The Bonn Convention is concerned with migratory animals; the Washington Convention, better known as CITES, is concerned with international trade in animals.

Unfortunately, any law is only as effective as its enforcers. This is a particular problem with international laws where so many different countries are involved, each with different interests.

> *The present (international law) situation leaves much to be desired. Certainly, the need exists for a truly global instrument with effective enforcement procedures.*
> Connecticut Journal of International Law

▲ *Richard Martin (who was responsible for the British anticruelty act of 1822) took Bill Burns to court for wounding his donkey.*

Speed can also be a problem with legislation:

> *It took 14 years to get a law prohibiting animal experimentation in elementary and high schools.* The American Society for the Prevention of Cruelty to Animals

Some people are dissatisfied with the law's ability to protect animals. Some people feel that violence is the only way to get things changed.

▶ *This photograph was used by the RSPCA in a poster campaign with the caption, "The only thing that's protected in this photograph is the man's identity." The law has been changed and foxes are now protected under British law.*

The end justifies the means?

Since 1977 there has been a rise in violence in the name of animal rights. Vandalism and bombs have caused damage costing millions of dollars.

❝ *On June 7 1990, Secretary Sullivan made headlines…by calling militant animal rights activists 'terrorists.'* **❞** *Congressional Quarterly*

In March 1995, the London Metropolitan Police's Special Branch set up a new group to investigate "animal rights terrorism." Was this a recognition of a darker side of animal protest, or an overreaction?

The FBI defines terrorism as "the unlawful use of force or violence against persons or property to intimidate or coerce a government, the civilian population, or any segment thereof, in furtherance of political or social objectives." Animal activists are only a small part of the world terrorism problem, but their extreme measures to protect helpless animals are still criminal actions.

❝ *We never had faith in the political system so used direct action to fight the many obscenities inflicted on the animal kingdom. We anticipate more will join the war being fought by so many good people outside the hopelessness of asking people with nasty habits nicely to stop destroying animals' lives. They insult humanity so deserve to be insulted and humiliated. They deserve more we think, soon they'll get it…. We only have to get lucky once.* **❞**

From statements signed by the animal rights group The Justice Department issued through the Animal Liberation Front Press Office

Victims of these "terrorists" have included scientists, retailers, farmers, chemists, and Prince Charles. Brian Cass, managing director of Huntingdon Life Sciences, was one victim. His UK company uses about 70,000 animals a year for research. Three masked attackers beat him with baseball bats in 2001, causing him physical injuries.

▲ This store was set on fire by animal rights activists to protest against the selling of fur coats. They put human lives at risk in order to help save animals.

◄ The people who protested about the export of live animals were prepared to risk their own freedom and even their lives for animal rights.

The number of people involved is very small (around 100 individuals in the Animal Liberation Front in the USA claimed responsibility for about 60 percent of incidents). But they make themselves known:

We can currently tune in on the Internet to a ten-page boast by the animal rights organization, the Justice Department. It lists some 150 people who have received potentially lethal missiles through the post. They are particularly proud of their latest weapon. It consists of a mouse-trap, welded to whose spring bar is a razor-blade coated with HIV-infected blood. Spectator magazine

The vast majority of animal groups distance themselves from any violence:

We're a moderate, middle-of-the-road organization. We would rather sit down at a table with people than throw paint at their doors. American Society for the Prevention of Cruelty to Animals

Activists who go to violent lengths regard themselves as crusading for animals. All movements have their radical supporters; we have to decide at what point acceptable forceful protest becomes unacceptable. Can it ever be right in a country with democratic elections for a group of people to use violence to try to change what they see as wrong?

▲ Antihunt saboteurs interrupt a foxhunt by trying to stop the foxhounds chasing the fox. This puts the horses, their riders, and the saboteurs in danger.

▲ The usual face of animal welfare groups is a peaceful one. Here, people line up to sign their protest in a streetside petition.

Rights for animals?

People's behavior toward animals is inconsistent. In the West cows are killed for food and dogs are kept as companions. But some people eat dogs in China. Many people who are opposed to experiments on animals would not be opposed to receiving medical treatment that had been developed through experiments on animals. Some people argue that humans are no different to any other animal, but reject human animal behavior, such as hunting.

Some people feel that the animal rights debate obscures the human rights debate.

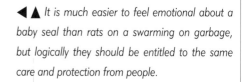◀▲ *It is much easier to feel emotional about a baby seal than rats on a swarming on garbage, but logically they should be entitled to the same care and protection from people.*

66 *I don't see the same moral outrage shown over animals being exhibited on the part of suffering humanity.* 99 *The Trouble With Animals, BBC TV*

66 *When a man has compassion for all living creatures, only then is he noble.* 99 *Buddha*

If we care about the suffering of animals, our first duty is to ensure they do not suffer. But people seem unable to agree on whether some animal suffering can be justified or whether animals have the right never to suffer. If animals have rights, we have to agree what those rights are.

Some argue it would be impossible for animals to enjoy exactly the same rights that humans do:

❝*The logical extension of animal rights is votes for oysters.***❞** *Bertrand Russell, 20th-century philosopher*

Others say that we are just too unimaginative or frightened to go the whole way and give animals full rights. A radically new approach is needed:

❝*It is not larger, cleaner cages that are called for in the case of laboratory animals, but empty cages; not more traditional commercial farms, but no commerce in animal flesh, whatever…. How we achieve these ends and whether we achieve these ends are largely political and educational questions.***❞** *Tom Regan, author of The Case for Animal Rights*

Rights come with responsibilities. Human rights have developed from deciding certain codes of acceptable behavior. Would we expect animals to abide by our rules? Would we take a cat to court for killing a bird, or prosecute a dolphin for killing a porpoise? We also have to decide where "life" begins and ends. If we

▶ *This bird has been caught in an oil slick. Since our world creates problems for animals, is it our responsibility to look after them?*

give animals rights, maybe we should give plants and lower organisms the same consideration.

Perhaps arguing about "rights" confuses the more immediate issue of animal suffering. A division has grown between people who believe in animal rights and those who believe in animal welfare. True animal-rights supporters object to both animal suffering and killing. Animal-welfare supporters object to animal suffering, but are prepared to accept animals are used by humans, whether for food, clothing, health, recreation, or companionship. Animal-welfare supporters believe animals have a right to be treated with respect and compassion, but not to be treated the same way as humans.

Most people fall into what American philosopher Strachan Donnelly calls "the troubled middle" on this. Where do you put yourself?

▼ *The natural world has its own laws: bears eat fish and fish eat flies. Where do humans fit in? Have our actions upset the natural order or merely changed it?*

Glossary

ANIMAL ACTIVISTS: People who take direct, and often militant action, in the name of animal rights.

ANIMAL WELFARE: Concern for animals' well-being and ensuring that they are not harmed or abused.

BATTERY HENS: Hens kept in stacks of cages in sheds and farmed intensively for their eggs.

BEHAVIORAL NEEDS: The basic conditions required for an animal to behave naturally.

BROILER CHICKENS: Young birds reared for food production.

BSE: Bovine Spongiform Encephalopathy, known as "mad cow disease." BSE-infected beef is thought by some people to be the cause of a similar brain disease in humans.

CULLING: Selective killing to remove the weakest/oldest animals to maintain stocks at a sustainable level.

ECOTOURISM: Tourism to places of ecological value. These are often conservation areas.

ENDANGERED: Any species whose numbers are so reduced it is in danger of being wiped out.

EXTINCTION: The complete disappearance of a species forever.

HALAL: Meat from animals that have been killed according to Muslim law.

HERBIVORE: An animal that feeds only on plants.

HUMANE: Compassionate (in this case toward animals); a humane killer is one that aims to kill an animal as painlessly as possible.

LOBBY: A group of people who try to influence lawmakers on behalf of a particular interest.

NATURAL SELECTION: Process whereby the strongest of a species is seen to survive and breed the next generation, at the cost of weaker members.

OMNIVORE: An animal that feeds on both vegetable and animal foods.

OVERWINTERING: Keeping animals inside during the winter.

PELTS: The name for skins of fur-bearing animals when they have been removed from those animals.

RENNET: Curdled milk found in the fourth stomach of a young calf, used for curdling milk to make cheese. It can also be made from the lining of the calf's fourth stomach.

SHECHITA: The Jewish method of killing animals for food.

SLAUGHTER BYPRODUCTS: Material left over from slaughtered animals once the edible meat has been removed, which is used to make other products.

SPECIESISM: A belief that animals are inferior to humans and can be used for human benefit without any regard to what they may suffer.

SUPEROVULATION: Artificially inducing a female animal to produce more eggs than would be produced naturally.

SUSTAINABLE HARVEST: A harvest that takes only what is needed in terms of resources while ensuring that stocks are not exhausted.

TERRORISM: The deliberate use of violence and terror to achieve an end (often political or religious).

VEGAN: A person who will not eat or use any animal products.

VEGETARIAN: A person who doesn't eat meat or fish or any other animal products, but will eat dairy products.

VIVISECTION: The performance of experiments on living animals.

Useful Addresses

Coalition to Abolish the Fur Trade
(CAFT)
P.O. Box 822411
Dallas , TX 75382
www.banfur.com

Doris Day Animal League (DDAL)
Suite 100
227 Massachusetts Ave, NE
Washington, DC 20002
www.ddal.org

EarthSave International
1509 Seabright Avenue
Suite B1
Santa Cruz, CA 95062
www.earthsave.org

Farm Sanctuary
3100 Aikens Road
Watkins Glen, NY 14891
www.farmsanctuary.org

Friends of Animals (FoA)
777 Post Road
Suite 205
Darien , CT 06820
Tel: 203-656-1522
www.friendsofanimals.org

The Fund for Animals
200 West 57th Street
New York, N.Y. 10019
Phone: (212) 246-2096
www.fund.org

Humane Society of the United States
(HSUS)
2100 L Street NW
Washington, DC 20037
www.hsus.org

In Defense of Animals
131 Camino Alto, Suite E,
Mill Valley, CA 94941
www.idausa.org

People for the Ethical Treatment of
Animals (PETA)
501 Front Street
Norfolk, VA 23510
Tel: 757 622 PETA (7382)
www.peta-online.org

Facts to think about

◆ Cosmetic tests on animals in Britain fell from 31,304 in 1980 to 1,319 in 1997, before being banned. In Europe, around 38,000 such tests are conducted each year. A poll conducted in the USA in 2004 found that nearly 75 ercent of Americans disagreed with animal experimentation in the cosmetics industry.

◆ The West indian communities of St. Vincent and the Grenadines are permitted by the International Whaling Commission to kill (strike) two Humpback whales each year.

◆ In the United States in 1949 the National Society for Medical Research found 85 percent of people favored animal research in laboratories. A National Science board survey in 1995 found 53 percent agreed with animal research. By 2004, according to several surveys, the approval figure for animal research was as low as 34 percent nationwide. And up to 25 percent of people wth chronic illnessses also disapproved.

◆ In Britain, 3 million people described themselves as vegetarian in 2003, a figure that has doubled in the last 10 years. About 2,000 more are added each week. And 7 million people said they no longer eat red meat, such as beef.

◆ Over 2 million whales were killed in the last century. Once there were 250,000 blue whales in the southern oceans; today there may be fewer than 1,000.

Index